WINGS OF HOPE

Meditations For
Daily Living

James R. Jacobson

James R. Jacobson
Publisher

WINGS OF HOPE

Library of Congress Catalog Card Number: 95-94164

ISBN: 1-55673-992-3   PRINTED IN U.S.A.

To all those places and people
who make my spirits soar:
a golden sunset over the ocean,
soul friends,
the laughter of children,
the mystery of growing things,
my garden,
my church,
the sacred found in common things and
Jesus the Christ of God.

Contents

Preface

The Psalmists wrote meditations for daily living. They used poetry to speak to the soul of a person. Listen to these paraphrased words from Psalm 19:1-4

How clearly the sky reveals God's glory!
How plainly it shows what God has done!
No speech or words are used, no sound is heard;
Yet God's voice goes out to all the world.

Jesus was able to hear God's truths while walking beside the sea or over the Judean hills. He was aware of the stars by night and the sun by day. He was at home in his Father's world.

Devotional time is a time of listening like Jesus listened and hearing like the psalmists heard. Wings of Hope may help you do this for yourself.

The most eloquent messages don't always come to us in words, but in our wonder as we see a sunset over the Grand Canyon or watch a little baby curl and uncurl her toes and beat the air with energetic arms.

Messages also come to us when someone throws loving arms around us and gives us a big hug. They come when a friend stretches out a helping hand when we're in trouble. Often no speech or words are used, but the message is heard in a way that lets us know, "God is in this place."

The helping hand you give your child,
The smile and love you give your wife,
Fulfills the daily call of God,
And brightens all of life.

J. Jacobson

Foreword

Isn't Sunday the time for expressing one's devotion to God? Isn't church the place where one's spiritual life is nurtured? Of course the church is important, but compartmentalizing our religious life actually runs counter to a realistic understanding of our Christian faith. To separate Sunday from the rest of the week and to draw hard lines between the sacred and the secular is to promote a dualism not found in the Bible.

"The earth is the Lord's and the fullness thereof, the world and all those who dwell in it" (Psalm 24:1). "For God so loved the world that he gave His only son" (John 3:16). These two well-known verses let us know that the whole world---not just it's parts---is the object of God's love and compassion

Dr. Jacobson's book of poetry and meditations helps the reader get beyond the dualism and compartmentalization of life and see the holy in everyday events. He appeals to us through the emotion of his poetry and the reasonableness of his meditations. I believe this book has a place in every reader's home.

Michael Pearson, Pastor
Dove of the Desert
United Methodist Church

Introduction

The language of the soul transcends verifiable knowledge and speaks in images, poetry and silence. Spiritual language witnesses rather than preaches. It is heard in rocks and trees, sky and sea, as well as in every relationship of life.

People find peace and wisdom in nature. Unfortunately this century has experienced an unprecedented exploitation of nature which has left us isolated and cloistered. Getting outside, making a garden, planting trees, all move us back to peace with ourselves, others, the world and God.

I see signs of hope as people are again looking for spiritual renewal. Many people are looking for spiritual depths, but fail to see God in the ordinary events of daily living. These meditations are an attempt to show *The Holy in the Common.* We see God in our daily tasks, in all our relationships and in nature. Our work, play, friendships, pleasure, and passion are all lifted to the level of the sacred. Grace, faith, hope and love are experienced on a daily basis.

This new attitude gives wings to our hopes. It is my prayer that a few minutes of meditation and prayer each day will renew your spiritual life and give you help, hope and healing.

The Holy in the Common

We meet the Holy in the common,
In the love of all of life,
In the joy of little children,
In growth through times of strife,

While we look to God in heaven,
God's spirit is right here,
In the burst of hearty laughter,
In the shedding of a tear,

No spoken word reveals God,
No written word describes,
For the word lived in a person,
Is the living word of life.
J. Jacobson

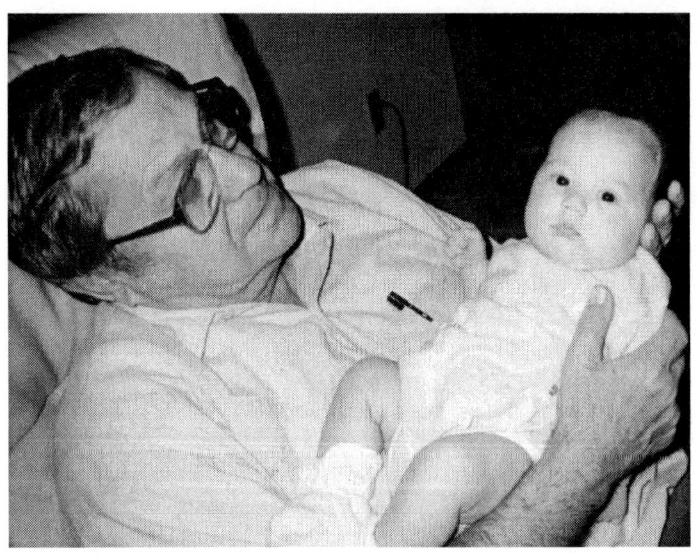

Scripture: Matthew 13: 55 *Is not this the carpenter's son? is not his mother called Mary? and are not his brothers James and Joseph and Simon and Judas?*

A young neighbor of ours went to the University and got his medical degree. He came back home to practice medicine. He lasted just a few years and moved on. His neighbors said, "Isn't this the boy who used to sell us minnows at the resort?"

Jesus had the same problem when he visited his home town. His neighbors dismissed him because they thought they knew him. They had watched him grow up and they knew his father, mother, and brothers. How could he have any special knowledge, for he was one of them. They dismissed the message by looking at the facts.

Today we let facts get in the way of seeing the possibilities in people. We miss the holy because we don't expect to see the holy in the common. We miss the holy in our children and our grandchildren because we know them. The wonder and mystery of life gets lost in the dust of daily living. Jesus was not able to do the wonderful works of grace in his home town because the facts of life prevented his neighbors from seeing the holy in the common.

Prayer. *Lord we often miss you because we let the facts of ordinary life cover up the holy. Open us to God's presence wherever it may appear. Amen.*

Thought: We meet the Holy in the common.

Soul Food

The soul is fed by poetry;
With music, verse and rhyme,
It grows with each experience,
That feeds the inner life.

Heaven can't provide the food,
That feeds the soul's desire;
It must be nurtured constantly,
Through memory, thought and action.

The food that gives the soul new growth,
Is personal for each of us;
It forms the character of one's life,
When freed from human barriers.

The soul is formed by quietness,
And voiceless urges from within;
It then transcends itself and us,
Through beauty, love and laughter.

The soul can guard a person,
Through darkness and despair;
It sees us through the sudden trials by fire,
And gives new life that's better than before.

There are no heights, there are no depths,
There is no solitude,
No place at all from which the soul's excluded;
Yet through the soul's expansiveness,
One transcends life itself,
And the gates of hell cannot prevail against it.

J. Jacobson

Scripture Matthew 6:25-26 *Therefore I tell you, do not worry about your life what you will eat or drink; or about your body, what you will wear. Is not life more important than food and the body more important than clothes? Look at the birds of the air; they neither sow nor reap nor gather in to barns and yet your heavenly Father feeds them.*

A major problem with the twentieth century is our obsession with things like food, clothing, cars, and homes. Our desire for these possessions leads to a loss of soul. When the soul is neglected it does not simply fail to develop, but rather it is filled with symptoms in us that are manifest as addictions, violence and a loss of meaning. The soul grows through its interaction with life.

Jesus suggests that it is easy for us to live in bondage to the common elements of daily life. Watch television for just a few minutes and you hear and see how easy it is to be attracted to the cultural messages of our day. We want success, attractiveness, and the good life. These elements may not be bad in themselves but they can block us from journeying toward God.

Prayer: *O God of kindness, we see the need for the care of souls all about us. A simple word of encouragement or a phone call to an aging parent. Let us not allow the dust of daily living smother our souls. Amen.*

Thought: The soul grows with each experience that feeds the inner life.

A Nurse

The one you call when you're in pain,
The one who comes to bring relief,
Then listens carefully to all complaints,
And shows compassion when she speaks.

A nurse is bound by real devotion,
To healing persons in need of care,
It matters not; race, creed, or background,
They all find comfort because she's there.

Her satisfaction is in a job well done,
Service to humanity makes it all worthwhile,
The nurse knows deep within her soul,
This task is one of hand and heart.

J. Jacobson

Scripture: Luke 6:36-37. *Be merciful, just as your Father is merciful. Do not judge and you will not be judged.*

An effective nurse needs compassion. To have compassion is "to feel with" another. *It matters not; race, creed, or background, They all find comfort because she's there.* Unlike mercy, compassion does not imply a superior/subordinate relationship. A compassionate nurse responds to the human face of a patient in need of care.

Another translation of Luke 6:36 reads, "Be *compassionate as your Father God is compassionate.*" Jesus' compassion expresses the radical nature of his message. It was more than an expression of the nature of God. Compassion is the core value of living together in a community. The message of Jesus was both personal and political. It was expressed in who he was and in what he did—he ate with sinners. The conflict of this social vision of Jesus has been lost in many churches and in our political structure, but it is still seen in a nurse who cares for a patient regardless of religion, race or background.

Prayer: *God of compassion, we miss the central quality of compassion in Christ and look more upon Him as judge than savior. We try to win purity in the sight of God and so fail to be compassionate as God is compassionate. Let us forgive others as you have forgiven us in Jesus. Amen.*

Thought: Be compassionate as your Heavenly Father is compassionate.

Breaking Out

I don't feel well inside my shell, I feel like hell!
Some day I'll break this awful shell,
And all the world will know and tell,
That I am doing well.

One day you came to crack my shell, I tried to yell,
"You're doing well, go ahead and crack my shell."
But then I thought,
"I don't hear well inside this shell,
How could you hear if I would yell?"

So I kept silent in my shell, I told myself,
"I'm really very comfortable and well,
Here all alone inside my shell."
I did not yell.

So now I'm stuck inside my shell.
I feel like hell!
I wonder why I didn't yell,
"Go ahead and crack my shell!"
                                    J. Jacobson

Scripture: Luke 5:19 *But finding no way to bring him in because of the crowd, they went up on the roof and let him down . . .into the middle of the crowd in front of Jesus.*

It's not always easy to get where you want to go in life. There are obstacles either of our own making or of the circumstances in life. Breaking out of our lot becomes discouraging so we draw into our shell. We want the fullness of life that God has for us, but we are afraid. It may be because of the crowd, or our condition. We want to break out and really live, but something always prevents us from making the move. We stay in our shell and complain about our plight.

Occasionally we need help from others in order to come to Jesus. We need others who can carry us up on the roof and let us down in the presence of Jesus. It is no disgrace to ask for help. Every one of us has needed support at times in order to break out of our shell. We all need the courage to yell, "Go ahead and crack my shell!"

Prayer: *O God of opportunity, I want to live in your presence with my life filled with the glory of the Lord, but I am afraid. I have let the modern world squeeze me into its mold. Give me a new glimpse of Jesus as I see how he was willing to break out of the limiting patterns of his day and live in freedom. Amen.*

Thought: We often need help to break out of our shell and come to Jesus.

Renewal

The clouds are almost broken up,
Blue sky comes shining through,
The rains have gone, the runoff's down,
And everything looks new.

The rains have brought the world to life,
The birds are singing in the trees,
There's harmony in their songs of joy,
As branches dance in desert breeze.

The rain, the sun, the birds and trees,
The freshness of the air,
Remind us of our Maker's love,
And of the thoroughness of God's care.

J. Jacobson

How wonderful O Lord are the works of Your hands!
The heavens declare your glory,
The arch of the sky displays Your handiwork.
In Your love you have given us the power,
To behold the beauty of Your world,
Robed in all its splendor.

Jewish Prayer

Scripture: Psalm 24: 1-2.

>*The earth is the Lord's and all that is in it,*
>*the world and those who live in it;*
>*for he has founded it upon the seas,*
>*and established it on the rivers.*

This summer while at the ocean with our grand children, I watched our four-year-old grandson roll in the sand, stand up and pick up handfuls of sand and let it sift through his fingers upon his shoulders. It was like a baptism as he became, "one with the earth," that covered him.

People find peace and wisdom in the out of doors. The psychological damage experienced by many of our children today comes to them because they are out of touch with the natural order. When one is in touch with creation, one is also in touch with the Creator. The Psalmists understood this and filled their poetry with sky, sea, thunder, rivers and streams. For them, the earth was God's holy place.

My wife and I go to the ocean at least once a year to find renewal. We also find it in the renewal of the desert after a rain and in the rising and setting of the sun.

Prayer: *Walk with me, O Lord as I look at the renewal of life that comes to us through your created order. Let me renew my own vision as I start to walk toward the light that has come to me through Jesus the Christ. Give me a vision of Christ that is so clear that I may experience life like a little child. Amen.*

Thought: God is found in the deepest rhythms of the universe.

One

No one lives alone and no one dies alone,
We are one body of humanity united with the world,
We are member's one of another,
Joined together in every moment of time,
If one member suffers all suffer,
If one rejoices all rejoice, for we are one.

The human family and created order are one,
The physical and spiritual are one,
I can not say of the air, "I have no need of you,"
Or of the land, water and trees, "I have no need of you,"
Plants and animals, sky and sea,
All are part of you and me, for we are one.

The physical spiritual balance is in us,
This makes living in the world special,
Our decisions make a difference to God and the world,
We create and destroy, relate and fracture,
We are in the world, and the world is in us,
We are in God and God is in us, for we are one.

J. Jacobson

Scripture: Mark 12:29-30. *When asked, "Which commandment is first of all?" Jesus answered, "The first is, 'Hear, O Israel, the Lord our God, The Lord is one." Love the Lord with all your heart and with all your soul and with all your mind and with all your strength.'. . . There is no other commandment grater than these."*

Recently we took our grandchildren, ages four and six, with us to the beach. The sheer joy of the children playing in the water and the sand was beautiful to watch. They ran in and out of the water with shrieks of joy. The older one rode the waves on a boogie board, while the younger one played in the sand and water and built sand castles with his grandmother.

Children are at home in the world. They feel the joy of being at one with the natural world. They don't separate God from the rest of life and they enjoy all of creation as a part of God's gift of life. Children seem to live and feel the meaning of that beautiful hymn, "All things bright and beautiful, all creatures great and small." The verse, " Each little flower that opens, each little bird that sings, God made their glowing colors, and made their tiny wings." This song comes to me when I see a hummingbird. Jesus prayed that his disciples may find the same oneness with God and the world that he had.

Prayer: *God of all life, Open our eyes that we may see you in the freshness of the air, the birds that sing and in the love we have for one another. Amen.*

Thought: We are one body of humanity, united with the world.

Joy

Joy is like the falling rain,
Refreshing all of life,
But we often miss this freshness,
When we're overcome by strife.
Refrain:
Freedom is the gift of Grace,
We have it through God's son,
in the coming of Christ the Lord,
The victory has been won.

Others also bring us joy,
We share each others pain,
When someone reaches out in love,
We can live again.
Refrain:

You create your own joy,
You know that you belong,
When others join you in a task,
You sing a freedom song,
Refrain:

J. Jacobson

Scripture: John 15: 11 *I have said these things to you so my joy may be in you and that your joy may be complete.*

The theologian, Paul Tillich wrote, "The experience of the suppression of joy almost drove me to break with Christianity. But he asked,—Is this because these groups are Christian or because they are not sufficiently Christian?"[1]

There is a universal search for joy, yet few find it because they miss the message of joy found in the coming of Christ. A pastor took his nine-year-old son to Disneyland for a special day. The father wanted to be a part of the son's joy in this exciting park. They took more than one trip down the Matterhorn and at the end of the day the father was tired. He said to his son, "Son I think it is time to go home." The son said, "I think Jesus wants me to have one more ride down the Matterhorn." The father asked, "How do you know?" The son said, "You taught me that Jesus is a part of all life. He was with me all day as we were having fun, and now I think he wants me to have one more ride down the Matterhorn."

The son had learned the father's lesson. Jesus brings joy to all life. He came to integrate our lives with all the rest of life. His coming brings great joy to all people.

Prayer: *God of joy and love, fill our hearts with your love as we experience the joy of life found in all creation, in our daily relationships with Christ our Lord and with others. Amen.*

Thought: Joy refreshes life.

---

1. Paul Tillich, The New Being. New York,
   Charles Scribner's Sons. 1955. 143

Grace

G *od gives us all the gift of grace,*
> *Through Jesus Christ his son,*
> *In the coming of our savior,*
> *Our freedom has been won.*

R *elease is found through this great gift,*
> *Grace frees us from all sin*
> *Through the coming of Christ Jesus,*
> *We can live and we can win.*

A *cceptance is a part of grace,*
> *We know that we belong,*
> *For the life we have in Jesus Christ,*
> *Lets us sing a freedom song.*

C *arefree as a little child,*
> *We want to sing and dance,*
> *For the coming of Emmanuel,*
> *Gives love another chance.*

E *ternity is with us now,*
> *All life has been made new,*
> *For the baby born in Bethlehem,*
> *Empowers me and you.*

So **GRACE** *brings all these gifts to us,*
> *It makes all life worth living,*
> *The God who comes to us in Jesus,*
> *Makes all of us more giving.*

J. Jacobson

Scripture: Ephesians: 2:8 *For by grace you have been saved through faith, and this is not your own doing, it is the gift of God.*

In John Steinbeck's book, *East of Eden* [2] the struggle of Caleb, the son, with Adam the father expresses the need for grace. Caleb seems to do everything wrong. He tried desperately to please his father and win favor with the father, but everything turned out wrong. He continues to try to make things right. He makes up for the loss his father suffered on lettuce by going into the wheat market. He makes money on the wheat only to be criticized by the father for exploiting farmers during wartime. The rejection by the father leads Caleb to destroy his brother, Aron.

Here is a parable of the ancient story of Cain and Able. Caleb like Cain, continues to want to work for grace and please the father by offering gifts. Like Cain of old, his gifts are not acceptable. Finally he comes to his father at the father's deathbed and cries, "I'm sorry father, I did it. I'm responsible for Aron's death and your sickness. I don't want to do bad things—but I do them."

Release comes through the gift of God's grace. We are released from the demand and from our guilt.

Prayer: *O God of grace, we seek release, but we think we must bring you something in order to be free. Help us see that you have accepted us just as we are. Thank you for listening to our cry for grace. Amen.*

Thought: Grace frees us from all guilt.

---

2. John Steinbeck. *East of Eden*
(New York. Viking Press, 1952) p. 602

Faith

F aithfulness is all of God,
He gave the world His Son,
Through the coming of the promised one,
Sin's power is overcome.

A ssurance comes to us through Christ,
It's ours when we believe,
God comes to us through Jesus,
And His promise is received.

I llumination comes from God,
Our darkness is made light,
Faith does not take life's task away,
It gives us new insight.

T rusting is a way of faith,
As you journey on your road,
The faith you have in Jesus Christ,
Helps you carry your own load.

H ope comes from our own having,
What our faith in God can bring,
The renewal of integrity,
Is worth more than anything.

So FAITH is part of daily life,
God's love is full and free,
Through the faithfulness of Jesus,
We've been given liberty.

J. Jacobson

SCRIPTURE: Galatians: 3:7 *You see that it is men and women of faith who are sons and daughters of Abraham."*
(Paraphrased for inclusiveness)

Faith has become a popular word in our society. We hear it on the radio and see it on television. We are told to have faith in the economic system. We hear football players exhorted to have faith in the coach and his coaching. Banners on stadiums read, "You have got to believe!"

There is another kind of faith that is different from these common expressions of faith. It is more than believing something about God, Jesus, and the world to come. Rather, it is entering into a relationship with the Christ to which the Christian tradition points. Faith means living out of this framework in life and placing God at the center of all life, as Jesus placed God in the center of his life.

Our faith is founded on the faithfulness of God and Jesus. This gives us a sense of assurance. It lets us say, *yes* to life in the face of all that would cause us to say, *no*. This kind of faith illuminates all life and leads to new life. Faith enables us to be born anew.

Prayer: *Dear Lord, today I am looking for the faith that lets me live and for that assurance that will carry me beyond my nagging doubts about myself, our institutions, and my own faithlessness. I know that your faithfulness is sufficient to draw me into a new relationship with you and others. Thank you for this faith. Amen.*

Thought: God's faithfulness is the foundation of our faith.

Hope

The future calls to us as hope,
With possibilities that are wild and free,
Like a butterfly, called into being from a chrysalis,
We break free and fly.

Our openness is part of hope,
We see small openings for new efforts,
And give birth to new efforts from small openings,
Our world is changed through us.

We become instruments of new values,
Transforming our small slice of history,
Step by step, through insight and creativity,
Hope opens the world to what it might be.

J. Jacobson

Scripture: Psalm 62:5 *For God alone my soul waits in silence, for my hope is from Him.*

Recently I counseled a women who was having trouble in her marriage. I heard a long recitation of faults and failures on the part of the husband. She said, "I've tried to tell him that he has to change or I am going to leave him." I asked, "Are there any good things that you enjoy about your husband?" At this she said, "Oh yes, he provides us with a good home, he is kind to the children and I still love him." I said to her, "Why not enjoy what you have together rather than concentrate on what you don't have."

Hope is born of openness. When we start to look for new possibilities rather than looking for faults, a relationship changes. When we see our wife or husband as a resource to be enjoyed rather than a problem to be solved, we can start to live in hope.

Hope for the Christian is anchored in the transcendent hope that God cares about us. His overreaching purpose calls us to new life as we hope in God. This kind of hope leads us back to living.

Prayer: *O God of hope, we come today in search of new life. We see possibilities that are wild and free. We fail in life because we are afraid. We want assurance in advance of each new venture. Help us live by God's promises, rather than wallow in our problems. Open us to the hope we find in Jesus. Amen.*

Thought: Hope opens the world to what it might be.

Love

God's love is freely given,
And Jesus is God's gift,
In Bethlehem when Christ was born,
God gave the world new life.

Our openness to God's great love
Enables us to live,
In Advent when we think of God,
We also want to give.

In Jesus, God was vulnerable,
God's son took on our flesh,
He lived among us while on earth,
In dying conquered death.

Eternity is with us now,
For Jesus walked our roads,
His presence lives on with us here,
And lightens all our loads.
J. Jacobson

Scripture: John 3: 16 *For God so loved the world that he gave his only son, that whosoever believes in Him may not perish, but may have eternal life.*

A child grew up in an orphanage until age six. She was then transferred to another orphanage, and finally to a third orphanage for transfer to an adoptive home in America. All attachments were torn away every few years so it became safer to avoid attachments and love.

Love is an attachment. Children need stability in their families in order to form a love bond. We can't just talk about love; we need to show it by doing loving things for each other. Jesus calls each of us to a new way of living in the world. It is a way motivated by love. To be in the Spirit of Christ is to express this kind of love in all our relationships.

We are like the Tin Man in *The Wizard of Oz*. We need a new heart. This includes a deepening relationship with the Spirit of God and greater love in our homes. Love is not a new set of requirements, but a total internal transformation brought about by centering all life in God. This is what Jesus taught by word and deed. He said: "You shall love the Lord your God with all you heart, soul, mind and strength." This is the essence of love for God.

Prayer: *O God of love and kindness, we see all around us the need for love—a simple word of encouragement, a phone call to an aging parent or a letter to a friend. Let us learn to love through deeds of kindness. Amen.*

Thought: Through deeds of love and mercy the Heavenly Kingdom comes.

Images

The Image that I have of God,
Can influence what I do,
If I see God as ruler King,
My choices then are few.

If I worship a "Big Daddy,"
That rules with iron hand,
I live in fear and not in love,
When life is hard to understand.

When I see God as loving parent,
Like my mother or my dad,
I feel the nurture care and love,
That makes my heart feel glad.

The God I see in Jesus,
Was a servant not a king,
He comes to me as loving friend,
And brings new life to everything.
J. Jacobson

Scripture: Colossians: 1:15 *He (Christ) is the image of the invisible God, the firstborn of all creation.*

A six-year-old friend wanted to draw me something. I suggested she draw me a picture of God. In a few minutes she showed me a picture of God with a clown's face and a hat. I said, "That's good, Kimber, but it looks like a man." She said, "I think God is a man." I asked, "What if God were a woman?" She replied, "That would change everything."

Kimber recognized the power of images—including our image of God. Our image of Jesus is often based upon the romanticized stories of the early followers. I call this the "blessed Jesus" image of the incarnation. It captures some of the truth found in these early writings, but often misses the images of liberation, journey and destination.

What is needed is a new image of Jesus which leads us to a dynamic understanding of His coming. This means that in Jesus, God has already done everything that needs to be done. We take steps toward the process of spiritual transformation into the image of Christ. Jesus showed us a new way of living in the world. We journey together toward the fullness of life God has prepared for us.

A second image from the life of Jesus, is a journey with a company of disciples. As followers, we live in a community that remembers and celebrates Jesus. Our communion service is our way of participating in his life.

Prayer: *Gracious God and Father of our Lord Jesus Christ, walk with us today on our journey through life. Keep us open to the fellowship of the gathered community so we may meet Jesus in the present moment of time. Amen.*

Thought: Jesus is the image of the invisible God.

The Winter of Life

We like to live in summer, with the sun's life giving rays,
We bask in all the sunlight that we can,
Then the frigid, icy winter comes to us with chilling force,
It shatters us, no matter what we plan.

No one escapes the bleakness of winter's frosty blasts;
There is no place where one can run and hide.
Yet it's the chill of winter where we find our life is cast,
These moments are the ones that will abide.

There are no heights, there are no depths, there is no solitude,
No place at all from which God is excluded,
God is standing in the shadows, and is calling you by name,
When you hear it, you know that you're included.
J. Jacobson

Scripture: Psalm 44: 17-18 *All this has come upon us, yet we have not forgotten you, or been false to your covenant. Our heart has not turned back, nor have our steps departed from your way.*

The Psalmists speak of the sunshine of life and of the chill of winter. God's people remain faithful in the good days and the bad. The riddles remain, but God is affirmed.

The unfair distribution of suffering in the world causes us to ask, "Why do the righteous suffer when they have done nothing to deserve it. Is God responsible for all the suffering?" There are no easy answers to these questions so we go on without answers.

The Psalmists insist that our hope comes from God who made heaven and earth. (Ps. 122:2) God is with us and suffers at our side. The outcome may not always be what we expected, but when we stay with God, His presence gives us hope in the winter of life.

Prayer puts us in touch with God. We do not ask for special favors, but come for the assurance that God is on our side. God's presence with us gives us the courage to go on in the bleak midwinter. We learn that we cannot drift beyond God's love and care.

Prayer: *O God, we often feel alone when we suffer. We long for the sunshine of life. We know that we cannot drift beyond your love and care. Our struggle, suffering and pain and our joy, pleasure and victory are shared by God. Nothing can separate us from the love of God in Christ Jesus. Amen.*

Thought: Nothing can separate us from the love of God.

God's Call

The call of God is forward,
Creating something new,
Through the courage of my action,
I respond through what I do,
I respond to God by giving love,
To one life has defeated,
Through my response, to my surprise,
I find I'm recreated.

The future opens as I risk,
I walk in ways unknown,
I follow my own inner call,
That's known to me alone,
Though the future is uncertain,
And it causes me to fear,
The God who walked with Abraham,
Is walking with me here.
J. Jacobson

Scripture: Revelation 21:5 *And the one who was seated on the throne said, "See I am making all things new."*

Jesus did not call us to be obedient to ancient laws, but to be free from the bondage of such laws. It was hard for Jesus' contemporaries to understand this. We respond to God by giving up the habitual, customary and socially approved actions and live in terms of a radically new future. God calls us forward.

Often Christianity comes across to people in terms of "don'ts." Is it any wonder that so many are attracted by the promises of the advertisers. We are told, "It's the real thing." The word, "new" is on every kind of product from soap to satellite dishes. These new ideas seem more attractive than "following the rules," and conforming.

The good news is simply this: God calls us forward. God calls us to a new future where we are open to a panorama of possibilities. We are called beyond the achievements of the past. We find this new life when we are able to risk the security of what is already established for a new future. The call forward opens each of us to a new life and we are empowered to bring new life to others.

Prayer: *Eternal God, we find it hard to let go of the past and we miss your presence in the call forward. Let us be open to the possibilities all around us as Jesus was open to Peter, the woman at the well, and Mary Magdalene. Amen.*

Thought: The call of God is forward, creating something new.

This Moment

Much of our religion directs us to the past,
And we miss the present moment,
In our search for what will last,
Our life flies by in moments,
That are given us each day,
And we wait for our salvation,
In a supernatural way.

We hang on to our dogmas,
To our creeds and to our songs,
While God calls us to service,
In correcting present wrongs,
There are deeds of love and mercy,
That need attention here,
In the living of this moment,
The Eternal draws us near.
J. Jacobson

Scripture: Mark 10: 15 *Truly I tell you, whoever does not receive the kingdom of God as a little child will never enter it.*

Children live in each moment. I never really understood the real meaning of Jesus' words until our son came home late for dinner one evening. His mother said, "David, you're late! What have you got to say for yourself?"

David said, "I know mother, and I'm sorry, but we saw so many interesting things. We were looking for grasshoppers so we could go fishing. While looking, we found an empty hornets' nest. We also found a dead dove and a dove's nest. It was so interesting we forgot about time."

Here a nine-year-old boy finds interest in grasshoppers, empty hornets' nests and a dead dove. I realized that this was the secret of Jesus' words: *...whoever does not receive the kingdom of God as a little child will never enter it.* Children see the wonder and mystery of life. They realize that the lived moment is the foundation of life. Each new stage brings a child new possibilities. A child is willing to risk the comfort of the old for the sake of the new. Christ's followers are asked to live fully in each moment of life.

Prayer: *Dear God, I may have missed you somewhere today. I may have rushed passed one of the new possibilities in life. Let me feel your presence in the warmth of a smile, a word of encouragement by a fellow worker, or the joy in a child's laughter. Amen.*

Thought: The lived moment is the foundation of life.

Creativity

I'm so secure in my own place,
Yet I would like to have more space,
I have the keys to outside doors,
Where life is found when one explores.

Why do I often sit inside,
And wish the world would open wide,
The doors of opportunity,
Where I would feel I'm really free?

Am I afraid to use my key,
Afraid of spontaneity,
Can novelty and growth in me,
Give life transforming ecstasy?

Or must I stay on safer ground,
And acquiesce to being bound,
By all my past conditioning,
Without one thought of listening?

I feel the urge to use my key,
And search for creativity,
Beyond the boundaries of my place,
Transforming life, through acts of grace.

J. Jacobson

Scripture: John 8: 36 *So if the Son makes you free, you will be free indeed.*

Some years ago, a leading industrialist said, "Say what you will, it is the profit motive alone that makes the wheels of the world go 'round." The profit motive is powerful, but freedom and creativity are the real values worth living for.

For me there is nothing more interesting than creating something that is valued by others. This innovation gives me a sense of freedom. It could well be creating a beautiful backyard or writing an article for the church. There is nothing more creative than parenting and now grandparenting. If we miss the joy of creativity, we miss a great deal of life.

Freedom is not found in having, but in being able to give something of yourself to others. The above scripture contrasts the position of a slave and a son in a household. Freedom implies a belief in the goodness and creativity of each person. One is nourished to explore, value and create when there is freedom. Freedom will give birth to new creativity, new art, new forms of self expression and a renewed interest in the beauty of the earth.

Prayer. *Lord, help us see that the work of Christ brings liberation to creation itself and opens us to creativity. Let us rejoice in this freedom. Amen.*

Thought: The call of God is forward, creating something new. Through the courage of our action, we respond through what we do.

He Took a Child

Life is hard and then you die,
It need not be this way,
Life can be good and you can grow,
On your journey day by day.

The end's the same for everyone,
We know that we must die,
So feel each moment while you live,
Create, laugh, play, enjoy,

Release the carefree child in you,
It's wondrous and it's wild,
When teaching others how to live,
Jesus took a child.

        J. Jacobson

Scripture: Luke 9:48 *Jesus took a child and said, "Whoever welcomes this child in my name welcomes me, and whoever welcomes me welcomes the one who sent me; for the least among all of you is the greatest.*

When an argument broke out as to who would be the greatest in the kingdom of God, Jesus took a child and had him stand beside him. He used the child to suggest the real meaning of the kingdom of God.

Most of us are like the disciples. We are looking for status and position in the kingdom of God. Jesus wanted to show that this was the wrong issue and he used a child for this lesson.

We need to look at the world through the eyes of a child. Our generation needs to learn the way of Jesus. His way is one of compassion rather than competition. It was a way of servanthood rather than one of supremacy, and it was a way of obedience rather than one of obstinacy. Through this teaching technique, Jesus suggested that the child represented the kingdom of God better than the disciples. The child was on a journey of transformation into something better while the disciples were looking for special favors.

Prayer: *Lord, help me see life through the eyes of a child. Let my life be transformed by the spirit of Christ who makes all things new. Amen.*

Thought: When teaching others how to live, Jesus took a child.

Born To Win

The stories' children write are not easily made new,
Lines that have been written are in everything they do,
They struggle to be free, they want to sing and dance,
They want the best of everything,
If they only had a chance.

An inner voice calls children, be the best that you can be,
But the story parents have written slows all efforts to be free,
They're bound by these old stories, it's hard to see new light,
So they stay with what is comfortable,
And complain about their plight.

Life calls children forward, rewrite what has been done,
Look beyond your isolation, the victory has been won,
Break lose and claim your freedom, re-center from within,
Let your own story tell the world,
You were born to win.

J. Jacobson

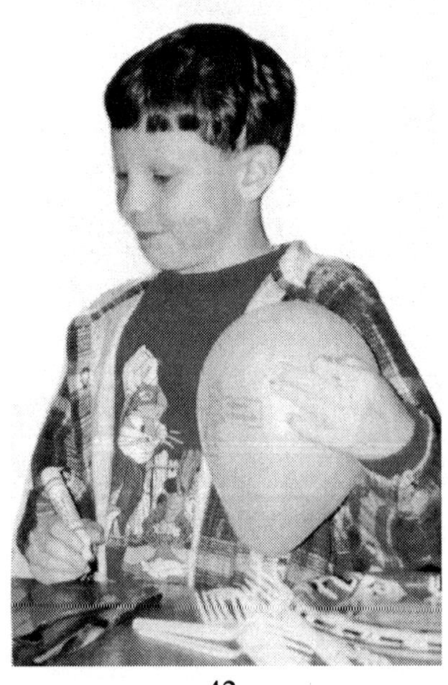

Scripture: Isaiah 11: 6 *The wolf shall live with the lamb, the leopard shall lie down with the kid, the calf and the lion and the fatling together, and a little child shall lead them.*

Recently, Gregory Kingsley, a twelve-year-old boy, sued to have all legal ties between his mother and himself severed so he could be adopted by his foster parents. He said, "I just want a place to be." Every child needs a place free from hunger, abandonment, violence and abuse. Every child is born to win, yet all around us we see losers.

This scripture gives us a picture of the harmonious companionship of animals and children. It is an image of the reconciliation of the world of nature and humanity. Perhaps this image is overly idealistic, but it lets us know that we must stop the enmity between nature and mankind. It points to a reversal of priorities where we place relationship before economic necessities. It lets us know that improvement in material circumstances comes through a new spirit among all people.

Children can help lead us into the new relationships when we give them a place in our lives, learn from children and release the carefree child in each of us. When we do this we will have more fun, enjoy life more and understand the nature of God's Kingdom better.

Prayer: *God of love, help us love with abandonment like a child. May we, like Jesus, give children a place in our lives and let a little child lead us. Amen.*

Thought: Every child is born to win.

Our Grandchildren

The wonder and mystery of life,
All wrapped up in our grandchildren,
New hope, new creative potential in three tiny tots,
We watch, listen and grow,
Memory and hope united in the grandparent's hearts.

Their words and motion, questions and wonder,
Have changed us and their parents,
They believe in us with all their hearts,
Their parents see their own families in a new way,
Our love for the grandchildren brings new family unity.

The mystery of birth and generations is experienced again,
We see the fathers, whose casualness can not hide their pride,
We see caring mothers whose intense love,
Confirms again the mystery of motherhood,
The heritage of countless generations is passed on.

Grandchildren are born and we are made new,
We await with excitement their emerging personalities,
As we see them reach for life, for love and joy,
In the world we have given them,
And a new generation is born.

J. Jacobson

Scripture: John 14: 23 *Jesus answered him, "Those who love me will keep my word and my Father will love them.*

After my mother died my father continued to come to Arizona each year to visit us. We felt sorry for him because we were so busy we could not spend much time with him. He told us, "Don't feel sorry for me, I have my memories."

Here, Jesus' earthly ministry is coming to an end. He tells his disciples that the spirit of truth will continue to guide them after he is gone. Jesus is made known to his disciples after his death by the quality of their relationship while he was with them. Each of us is inevitably affected by the lives of our parents and grandparents.

Grandparents can be models of unconditional love for their grand children. We enjoy our visits with our grandchildren. We laugh more, play more and work together better as husband and wife when our grand children are with us. They put us back in touch with life and we sprinkle stardust over their lives as they give us new life, filled with memory and hope.

Prayer: *God of hope, we come today to pray for our grand children. Let our relationships with them express your love, that the mind of Christ may be formed in them. Amen.*

Thought: Grand parents both give and receive new life from their grandchildren.

My Task

There are no easy answers to the questions that life asks,
And finding divine guidance has its flaws,
But we can live each moment, while doing daily tasks,
And we can find transcendence in our cause.

Heaven can't give meaning to the work we do each day,
For meaning is not given from above,
It comes to us each moment through what we do and say,
It comes to us when we're transformed by love.

There is intrinsic value in each moment and each day,
The decisions that we make form us and God,
We live the values that we have by how we do our task,
And some will criticize and some applaud.

J. Jacobson

Scripture: Luke 22: 28 *"You are those who have stood by me in my trials; and I confer on you, just as my Father has conferred on me, a kingdom."*

This scripture comes at the close of Jesus' earthly ministry. He is letting his disciples know that each one of them has a kingdom. The idea of the "kingdom" is fundamentally one of "sovereignty" or "rule." It often refers to a future reality, but it is clear that Jesus intended to let his disciples and also you and me know that each of us has been given an area of responsibility in life. Each one of us has been given a task.

The kingdom refers to a future time, but Jesus also speaks of the kingdom as already present. Just as the cross was not to be separated from Jesus' earthly ministry, the future kingdom can not be separated from the disciples earthly task. The disciples' response to the challenge of the earthly task determines their place in the future kingdom. What was true for the disciples is also true for us, for each of us has been given a task to fulfill in our time.

Prayer: *Gracious God, we cannot believe you have made us but to die and inherit a kingdom. Help us see your hand in our daily task and give us the courage of our faith to fulfill this task. Amen.*

Thought: We live the values that we have by how we do our task.

The Sands of Time

The sands of time are falling,
Into my life today,
The moment I am living now,
Will quickly pass away.

Today confronts me with a task,
I can accept or turn aside,
But once the falling sand is past,
The choice I make must then abide.

I can not halt or slow the sand,
It flows each moment on its way,
But I can use my moments now,
To find God's purpose for this day.
                    J. Jacobson

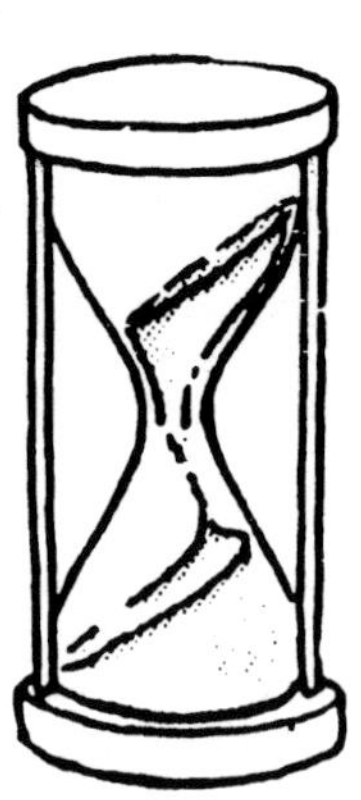

Scripture: Ecclesiastes 3: 1-3 *For everything there is a season, and a time for every matter under heaven: a time to be born, and a time to die; a time to plant, and a time to pluck up what is planted; a time to kill, and a time to heal; a time to break down and a time to build up.*

Years ago I was involved in teaching salesmen. We instructed them to find the right prospect, at the right time and do and say the right things. The key to sales was, "the right time." Jesus came, "at the right time." Our scripture suggests that there are milestones along the road of life. We journey on to meet them at the appointed hour.

We live and move and have our being in appointed patterns much too vast for us to understand. Our adjustment to these conditions is found in our wisdom or our foolishness in our daily decisions.

This scripture does not raise the questions of freedom and choice or our responsibility in life, but rather clearly defines the limitations under which we live. The reconciliation of the circumstances of life with the limitations comes as we understand, not only our freedom, but also our limitations.

Prayer: *O God, Give me honest discontent with the way things are in my own life. Make me aware of the limiting scripts that I have written for myself or discovered in life. Let me see my task when it comes and give me the courage to say "yes" at the right moment. Amen*

Thought: Today confronts me with its task, I can accept or turn aside.

DEPRESSION

I'm really depressed and I don't know just why,
Was it the funeral, but all of us die,
I've been there before and laid friends to rest,
I was not discouraged nor was I depressed.

Perhaps it's the cost of repairs on the car,
A dollar today doesn't go very far,
Or was it the pool I had to repair
I do like to swim, and spend my time there.

Or is it the people reporting the news,
On taxes, character, haircuts and shoes,
They talk and they talk, but little is said,
I guess all their speaking has gone to their head.

They cover up issues a blind man can see,
The forgotten people are now you and me,
Will someone deliver us from this whole mess,
Or will the news people just talk and depress.

J. Jacobson

Scripture: Psalm 42:11 *Why are you cast down, O my soul, and why are you disquieted within me? Hope in God; for I shall again praise him, my help and my God."*

We are living in disquieting times, and the news media often adds to our depression. We seldom read a newspaper without learning of more bad news. Our elected officials campaign on negatives, rather than on signs of hope. Is it any wonder that some of the fastest selling drugs are anti-depressants?

The constant barrage of negative news and the rehashing of these stories is a source of sorrow in our time. Our souls are disquieted within us. We often feel the pain of our own anxiety and wonder where we can find deliverance. The God whom we once felt was near now seems far off. We feel forgotten and oppressed.

When my soul is cast down within me, I can continue to hope in God. This is a deeper concern than the kind of hope a person has when looking for a job. Hope in God gets me beyond the problems of daily living to a transcendent hope. When one has this kind of overarching hope, the problems of the day, including the news people who depress, can be managed.

Prayer: *God of hope, we are often disquieted in our spirits by the dust of daily living. We wonder, ''Can we hope again?'' We can go on because our hope is in God. Thank you God, for this hope. Amen.*

Thought: Hope is essential for daily living.

We Let Her Go

I see her going now,
That little girl so beautiful but bewildered,
When she came to us, out of the blue,
From that land beyond the sea.

So naive and innocent, about America and our ways,
So full of life and hope—
A bundle of potential all tied up,
In a tiny ten year old .

How could ten short years change her so?
How could she learn our language, finish our schools,
And become so one with us,
In ten short years?

She is going from us now, and we must let her go,
We fear she is not ready,
Yet she must go to life, to new growth,
In her adopted land.

We struggle to take our hands off her,
To let her learn from others, in new relationships.
We feel both joy and pain as she goes,
And we let her go!
J. Jacobson

Scripture: John 11:44b. *Jesus said to them, "Unbind him, and let him go."*

Some years ago we adopted a daughter from Korea. She was with us for ten short years when she moved out and married. It takes time, courage and trust for parents to let their children go to life. On occasion you simply stand back and hold the bandages and ointments ready.

This scripture is filled with symbolic language with the resounding call to Lazarus, "come out!" His hands and feet were bound with strips of cloth, and his face wrapped in cloth. There is a second command, "Unbind him." This lets us know we have a task in fulfilling Christ's command. Finally there is a third command, "Let him go." This is where we often fail. We may help free someone, but then bind that person again to a cause of our choosing.

When it comes to our own call, we often hear the voice of God, but only stir a little. We're satisfied with our limited interests in our tomb. We miss the fullness of the life Christ has to offer. We sometimes let others unbind us only to be bound again by some habit of culture or tradition. We have trouble letting our children go to life.

Prayer: *God of hope, it is hard to let go of those we love. Let us know that those whom you have bound to us, can also go from us. We believe that when you start a good work in a person, it will go beyond our own control. Amen.*

Thought: "Unbind him and let him go!"

Izumi

She is getting married today,
Our exchange student so vital, but bewildered,
When she came to us, out of the blue,
From that land beyond the sea.

So guileless and innocent about our culture;
So full of life and hope—
A bundle of potential,
All tied up, in a seventeen year old student.

How could one short year change her so?
How could she learn our language,
Graduate from our schools,
And become so one with us in one short year?

She is getting married in her own country.
We have traveled to her homeland,
To celebrate with her and her new husband,
On this, their special day.

We share this exciting day, with her birth parents,
As we learn to know them for the first time,
Ecstatic together, across cultural lines,
And all our lives have been enriched.

J. Jacobson

Scripture: Galatians 3:28 *There is no longer slave or free, there is no longer male and female; for all of you are one in Christ Jesus.*

A few years ago we invited Izumi Yamamoto, an exchange student from Japan, into our home. She spent a year with us, finished high school and became an important part of our family. She has visited us twice since then and recently invited us to her wedding.

We went to Japan for her wedding and spent eleven delightful days with Izumi and her family. We stayed in her home, ate their food and slept on the floor, Japanese style. When Izumi left for her honeymoon we spent several days with her parents with an English/Japanese dictionary in hand, laughing and sharing both our culture and family histories. It was one of the great experiences of our life as we discovered the oneness of families in different cultures.

The above scripture takes on new meaning as we learned again the universal nature of the spirit of Christ. There is no male or female, American or Japanese, but one body of humanity united by a common love.

Religion often becomes a stumbling block toward the realistic handling of different cultures. If one lives in the spirit of Christ, human problems have a way of dissolving. All races and cultures meet in him as the rivers of the world meet in the sea. We experienced this in Japan.

Prayer: *God of hope and joy, let us reach out to others in love. Help us see your presence in the celebration of a wedding even when that wedding is in another country and another culture. Amen.*

Thought: "In Christ there is no East or West."

Families

We're all born in families,
And our families live in us,
Their stamp is clearly visible,
In eyes, in height, and hair.

Don't worry about your heritage,
You can't change it if you tried,
Don't fret about what you don't have,
Secure the gifts you're given.

Use the talents that you have,
Develop all your skills,
Don't blame your parents or others
For the times when you have failed.

Seize every opportunity,
You meet along the way,
Find the adventure in each task,
Expand each new horizon.

Your family can not limit you,
Without your own permission,
So let them know right from the start,
You have your own commission.

J. Jacobson

Scripture: Proverbs 23: 25 *Let your father and mother be glad; let her who bore you rejoice.*

Concern for family relationships is as old as the history of the human race. Today the new mobility of society and the rapid social changes that have come about through industrialization, urbanization and working moms have brought families a new set of problems. Father's and mothers are not always glad about family relationships.

Religion is still evident in many homes, but it is ordinarily not considered as a primary factor in running the household. The church exists alongside other service and sports organizations as a "place to go" rather than a source of family values.

Both this scripture and our own experiences tell us that the greatest joy that parents can have is wise and sensible children. The training must start early when children are impressionable. Children need to be encouraged to be all that God intended them to be through both inheritance and opportunities. Each child has a mission in life, and it is his or her task to find and fulfill it.

Prayer: *God of all life, we pray today for the life of our families. Let us remember that the followers of Jesus' way are also models for others who are just finding their way. Make us living models of Christ's way for our children. Amen.*

Thought: The parents of the righteous will rejoice.

Waiting

Waiting for the phone to ring,
When trying to sell a horse,
Waiting for the lawyers,
When getting a divorce.

Waiting to be seated,
When you go out to eat,
Waiting in the post office,
While standing on your feet.

Waiting in the doctor's office,
When you're all out of sorts,
Waiting for the mail to come,
And for the lab. reports.

Waiting to board the plane,
When traveling by air,
Waiting in the complaint line,
Arguing about the fare.

We spend our lives in waiting;
Why not live instead?
Or we may spend our final days,
Waiting 'til we're dead.

J. Jacobson

Scripture : Isaiah 40:31

> *But they who wait for the Lord shall renew their*
> *strength,*
> *They shall mount up with wings like eagles,*
> *They shall run and not be weary,*
> *They shall walk and not faint.*

There are two kinds of waiting. There is an empty waiting like that in a doctor's office when we are expected to read old magazines and catch up on old news. The waiting found in our scripture is a kind of waiting that is filled with expectation. We stop fighting life and let it come to us.

It is hard for us to wait expectantly. We want to be doing something. The world can not offer itself to us while we are on the run. This beautiful poem of Isaiah points to a radically different kind of waiting. "They that wait upon the Lord shall renew their strength." This kind of waiting is contrasted with the ambitious campaigns of society in the prophet's day and in ours. Waiting for the Lord can renew us, as we see the gracious power of God in historic events.

When we wait upon the Lord, we learn that God has a hand in the victories of the day. He is working to shatter the forces that bring bondage. He renews our strength.

Prayer: *God of all life, we are so impatient in our search for the fullness of life. We want things done yesterday. Give us the patience to wait upon the Lord so that we may renew our strength. Amen.*

Thought: They that wait upon the Lord shall renew their strength.

Work

We must work for years and years,
To find a peaceful place to rest,
Then often find without a task,
We feel there's something missing.

The poetry of the work we do,
Gets lost in tools and training,
Without fulfillment from our work,
We're lost in daily functions.

Our hopes and dreams must be expressed,
In office, store and factory,
We craft a self through daily toil,
That feeds our soul's desires.

The spirit that sustains our work,
Expresses who we really are,
Our work is offered up to God,
With pride and satisfaction.

J. Jacobson

Scripture: Genesis 2:15 *And the Lord God took the man and put him in the garden of Eden to till it and keep it.*

The poetry that has God "walking in the garden" when taken literally seems childlike and naive. When understood symbolically we learn that it is the nature of God to appear. We can fashion many things through our work, but only God gives us that on which all life depends.

A second image found in our scripture is that we must till the ground. We would like the fruit to fall from the trees, but this is not the way of life. We learn that though we create nothing, we are responsible for the cultivation of the earth.

Jesus talked about the natural order a great deal. "Behold a sower went forth to sow" (Matt. 13:31). Often our urban civilizations lose the understanding of growth and the cooperation it takes to have a garden. I use my back yard and garden for spiritual renewal. I feel the oneness of all life and my place in growing things as I "till" the soil. This is wisdom we learn from nature.

Prayer: *Creator God, we have often suppressed the natural, and failed to see our place in the care of the earth. Let us learn that planting and caring for a garden move us back to living in harmony with all life. Amen.*

Thought: Without fulfillment from our task, we're lost in daily functions.

The Shadow of Death

The grief of death has sapped my strength,
I'm numb confused and frightened,
The one so dear to me is gone,
And I'm left empty and alone.

This mortal wound is felt so deep,
It's like a part of me has died,
Something within me now must end,
My soul now wanders from it's home.

The mysteries of life and death,
The pain and grief I feel inside,
Cause me to wonder and to cry,
And contemplate the question, "Why?"

Is it God's will that I must lose;
The one that meant the world to me?
God does not take our love from us,
I'm sure God suffers in our loss.

Death's shadow falls on all of us,
It comes in ways too deep for words,
Yet I'm assured within my soul,
My grief is carried in God's heart.

J. Jacobson

Scripture: Psalm 23:4

Even though I walk through the darkest valley,
I fear no evil; for you are with me;
your rod and your staff— they comfort me.

Those of us who have lived any length of time know that sorrow, sickness and death are a part of life. These experiences are as real as love, joy, beauty and happiness. Death is one of the most difficult hardships for any of us to face. The soul is sick and needs to be restored. This scripture brings comfort and hope to people who have suffered a loss. It uses a simple technique with a shepherd guiding us on our journey.

For the Christian, Jesus is the shepherd who leads us beside the still waters and restores our soul. We rest in green pastures and walk in paths of righteousness. The journey is not haphazard because we have a guide. We believe in our guide, and need not fear anything in life or in death.

The imagery of this great Psalm carries us beyond life itself. It lets us know the Lord God will never abandon us.

Prayer: *Almighty God, we thank you for all the experiences of life. Help us see you in moments of disappointment, pain and suffering as well as in the days of joy. When words of thanks die upon our lips, help us see that a new day will come when we can thank you for the dark days as well as the bright. Amen.*

Thought: I'm assured within my soul, my grief is carried in God's heart.

Good Friday & Beyond

Christt my redeemer on Calvary bled,
He suffered there on the cross,
They planted a crown of thorns on his head,
But obedience to God was not lost.

The world of his day did not understand,
The way of compassion He taught,
The power of evil arrayed against Him,
Was more than His followers thought.

Jesus came to earth to set us all free.
He lived what He really believed.
Conventional wisdom was shown to be wrong.
Deliverance could now be received.

He is seated today at the right hand of God,
He calls us again to be free,
This image let's everyone know that He lives,
At God's side where He now intercedes.

J. Jacobson

Scripture: Romans 8:26 *Likewise the Spirit helps us in our weakness; for we do not know how to pray as we ought, but that very Spirit intercedes with sighs to deep for words.*

Some years ago a mother lost a son in an accident. She asked, "Why did God do this to my son?" Many of us expect God to control everything, but this would make us puppets on a string. The free obedience of thinking people is more valuable than being a puppet. Most of us agree with this, yet when it comes to prayer we either tell God what to do or expect God to direct us.

Prayer can not be separated from the rest of life. It must correspond to what we believe about God and the world. Prayer starts with a belief that there is unity in life. It is a recognition that in God we live and move and are. When we live in this way we know that Christ's spirit intercedes for us in ways we can not express.

We often think of the life, death and resurrection of Jesus, but fail to recognize that he now intercedes in our behalf. This takes us beyond Good Friday and Easter.

Prayer: *Gracious God, we don't know how to pray in accord with what must be, but we know that Jesus is praying in our behalf. We know that the Spirit found in Jesus when he walked our roads is with us now. Thank you for this assurance. Amen.*

Thought: The Spirit found in Jesus intercedes in my behalf.

The Resurrection

I've denied my Lord like Peter,
And I have my doubts as well,
I often feel like Thomas,
With unbelief to dispel.

Has Jesus really come alive?
I don't know how to feel,
How do we know He's living now?
Can this story still be real?

The resurrection dawns on me,
In ways to deep for words,
I see new light upon my path,
Experienced as the Lord's

I start anew like Peter,
I believe beyond my doubts,
I celebrate God's presence here,
With Easter's joy and shouts.

I live in Easter's afterglow,
Beauty blossoms like a rose,
I sing a song of triumph,
Hallelujah! Christ arose!
                    J. Jacobson

Scripture: John 21: 12 *Jesus said to them "Come and have breakfast." Now none of the disciples dared to ask him, "Who are you?" because they knew it was the Lord.*

Some years ago I played "Father Christmas" in a drama. Later I saw a picture of myself in costume and wondered, "Who is this person?" This is what the disciples wondered about the resurrected Jesus.

The resurrection dawns on us in many ways that can not be expressed in words. If we try to force all of the language of the resurrection and appearances of Jesus into scientific and rational terms we will lose the meaning of Jesus' presence with us today.

These scriptures let us know that Jesus came to the disciples while there were doing their common task. Christ can find us in the work place as truly as at the altar. The spiritual life and everyday life are never split apart in the life and teachings of Jesus.

When we see the earth as the sanctuary of God and give ourselves to maintaining the earth as well as human life we will again discover the power of the resurrection. When we see our task in this way, the resurrection will dawn on us in ways too deep for words, and our work will again have dignity.

Prayer: *God of all life, let me feel the power of the resurrection in my daily task. Help me recognize Jesus when he appears to me and asks for breakfast. Amen.*

Thought: The resurrection dawns on me in ways too deep for words.

Released for Living

Lord I worry and complain,
I live under constant strain,
And I cannot see the glory of the Lord,
Life is crowded to the hilt,
With the things that we have built,
And I feel like I've become a mere machine.
Refrain:
Release my body free my soul,
Re-unite me, make me whole,
Set me free Lord, and let me live again.

Free my spirit, free my mind,
Let me serve you through mankind,
Let the light of the eternal fill my soul
Give me knowledge that's secure,
And a peace that will endure,
In a world where both seem harder to sustain.
Refrain:

Let God's grace renew my heart,
Set me free to do my part,
Let the joy of Christ return into my soul,
Let the power of God's great love,
Come to me as did the dove,
Come to Jesus by the Jordan long ago.
Refrain:

Let Christ's Spirit fill my life,
Let it drive away all strife,
Make me new Lord in a true creative way,
Let my body, mind and soul,
Be united and made whole,
By God's spirit which gives unity to life.
Refrain;

Scripture: Galatians 5:1 *For freedom Christ has set us free. Stand firm, therefore, and do not submit again to a yoke of slavery.*

Every society relies on families to transmit its values, culture, and traditions. The value of freedom is rooted deep within the human soul. It is very strong in teens who want what they want whenever they want it. They have not caught the message of Paul that lets us all know that freedom includes self-regulation.

J.B. Phillips captures the dangers of our secular culture in his translation of Romans 12:2. *"Don't let the world around you squeeze you into its own mold, but let God re-mold your minds from within, so that you may prove in practice that the plan of God for you is good, meets all his demands and moves toward the goal of maturity."*

It is so easy to be captured by the social climate of our day where the good life is found in having things. We become enslaved by the advertisers who try to make us believe that happiness is in having the right automobile, home or the right food and drink. Gradually we are squeezed into conformity with the dominate culture and lose the freedom which is ours in Christ.

Prayer: *God of all life, we are surrounded by forces that try to squeeze us into a mold. The advertisers try to sell freedom, but it leads to bondage. Let the freedom of Christ come into our homes in all its power so we may follow his way of freedom. Amen.*

Thought: Don't let the world around you squeeze you into its mold.

Church Meetings

The Church's one foundation, is meetings every day,
This is our new creation, to wile our time away,
From meeting we are coming, to meeting we must go.
We spend our time together, but still the church won't grow.

We toil through tedious speeches, from those who run the show,
They say that we must labor, to make our programs go,
Yet from our several meetings, we go our separate way,
To wait the next reminder, to meet another day.

Yet meetings are important, we know that we must go.
If we would make our journey, upon this earth below,
For when our journey's over, St. Peter then will say,
"Do you have your agenda, for the meetings of the day?"

J. Jacobson

Scripture: Matthew 16: 16 *Simon Peter answered, "You are the Messiah,(Christ) the son of the living God."*

One day I came home from three days of meetings and sat down and wrote this poem on church meetings. It is easy to replace Christ with daily meetings. I wrote this poem to remind myself of the ease in which I replace what I ought to do with what I'm doing.

This affirmation by Peter,"You are the Messiah," has caused controversy in the church since early days. It is evident that Peter himself didn't understand what he meant when he said it. He didn't understand that Jesus must suffer and die. When Jesus tried to teach the disciples this truth Peter objected, and Jesus rebuked him with the words. "Get behind me Satan."

It is easier for us to attend meetings than to put ourselves in the service of Christ without reservation. There is a danger in being followers of Christ for we must be willing to deny ourselves and take up a cross and follow. We must be willing to lose life in the struggle against evil for the sake of Christ.

Prayer: *Gracious God, keep us from replacing the challenge of Christ with things that we do. Help us center life in God rather than in church meetings. May we capture the Spirit of Jesus and discover the sacred in the ordinary. Amen.*

Thought: Each individual is responsible for justice and righteousness in the land.

The Holy in Communion

We meet the Holy in communion,
In the bread and in the wine,
In the food from golden grain fields,
And the fruit from off the vine.

While we look to God in heaven,
God's spirit is right here,
In our gathering for communion,
Christ's spirit draws us near.

No spoken word reveals God,
No written word describes,
Like the Word that's found in Jesus,
As God's living word of life.

Communion is the most dramatic way for us
to experience the Holy in the common.
Our communion service reminds us of this meeting.

Pour out your Holy Spirit on us gathered here,
and on these gifts of bread and wine,
Make them be for us the body and blood of Christ,
that we may be for the world the body of Christ,
redeemed by his blood.

(The United Methodist Hymnal p. 14)

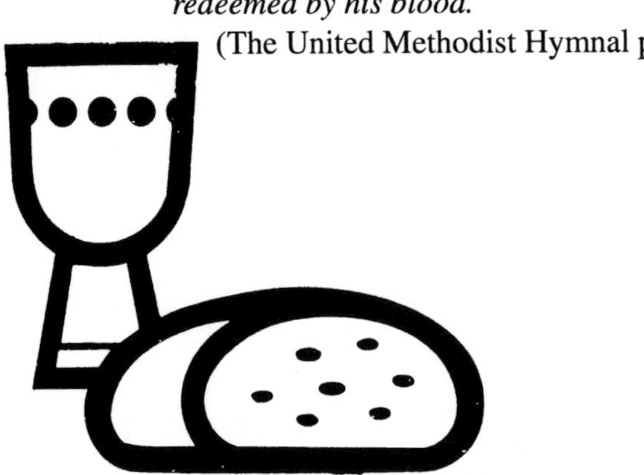

Scripture: Luke 22: 19-20 *Then he took a loaf of bread and when he had given thanks, he broke it and gave it to them saying, "This is my body, which is given for you. Do this in remembrance of me." And he did the same with the cup after supper, saying, "This cup that is poured out for you is the new covenant in my blood."*

The holy and the common meet in our communion service. The holy is carried through the grain from off the fields that is made into bread and sustains life. The fruit of the vine gives us refreshment. We are sustained by both food and drink.

This event in the life of the disciples is more than a symbol. It is an act of Jesus that was remembered by the early church and passed on to us as a Sacrament. It is given to help us remember the risen Christ.

There is a second element in communion which we may miss. It lets us know that Christ is made manifest in our eating and drinking together. The ordinary, the bread and the fruit of the vine, are lifted to the level of the sacred. We become the body of Christ for the world, redeemed by his blood.

Prayer: *Merciful God, we have failed to be your body in the world. We have not done your will, we have rebelled against your love and have not loved our neighbors. Forgive us, we pray and free us for joyful obedience through Christ our Lord. Amen.*

Thought: In the gathering for communion, Christ's spirit draws us near.

One in Ten
From Luke 17: 11-19

They walked the roads together,
Their hands and feet destroyed.
The face of death was on them,
No one could be employed.

Ten Lepers stood their distance,
As Jesus passed their way.
They all cried out for mercy,
Hoping for a better day.

Jesus showed compassion,
As he sent them to the priests.
All ten were cleansed of leprosy,
As God's power was released.

Just one returned to give God thanks,
And he was not a Jew.
This outsider from Samaria,
Seemed to know just what to do.

So one in ten was grateful,
Because he was made whole.
The other nine quickly forgot —
And showed their lack of soul.

J. Jacobson

Scripture: Luke 17: 15-18 *Then one of them when he saw that he was healed turned back, praising God with a loud voice and fell on his face at Jesus' feet and he was a Samaritan. Then Jesus said, "Were not ten cleansed? Where are the nine? Was no one found to return and give praise to God except this foreigner?"*

I remember a vacation Bible school lesson when I was five or six. The teachers passed out candy during a break. Each child was given a piece of candy. They were then lined up according to the child's response. The children who said, "Thank you," were directed to one line and the rest of us were put into a second line. The children who said, "Thank you," were given a second piece of candy. I was in the line that failed to give thanks. What an embarrassment! My mother had taught me better, but I failed to give thanks for a simple gift.

Our scripture lets us know that one in ten was grateful and he was the outsider. Isn't it strange that the outsider often becomes the hero in Jesus' stories? The seed of gratitude must be in a person before it can grow. Praise should be as natural to men and women as songs are to birds. We, like the nine, miss a great deal in life because we fail to give thanks. I missed a second piece of candy when I was a child, but I have learned that I miss much more when I fail to express gratitude to God for the goodness of life.

Prayer: *Gracious God, forgive us for our ingratitude. You have given us all we need for life, happiness and healing. Give us one thing more — a grateful heart. Amen.*

Thought: Thankfulness feeds the soul.